***Job Festered...***

I itch.

My One,
I do not understand.
I drink the story of Abraham
and hold it between my teeth
wishing it would hatch
and the pretty bird
would fly.

The **3** Faces of Brahman

# The 3 Faces of Brahman

**Christine O'Leary-Rockey**

**PostDada Press**

Copyright © 2010 Christine O'Leary Rockey
All Rights Reserved

ACKNOWLEDGMENTS: The following poems have appeared in
*The Fledgling Rag, LitChaos,* and *Megeara*: "A Love Song in Gray Morning",
"Sonata 85", "Concentric (or Allah in Circles)",
"Electra: From the Closet", "Mercury in Retrograde", "The Wisdom of
Delilah". The author is grateful to the editors of these publications and to the
good people who helped to put this book together.

Cover Design and Photography: Erin Sparler
Back Cover Photography: Macrina Newhouse
Editorial Assistance: Jeanette Trout
Typography and Layout: Erin Sparler

PostDada Press:
Harrisburg, PA and Baltimore, MD
www.PostDadaMedia.com

ISBN: 1-879294-56-7

## *Foreward*
by Michael Lear-Olimpi

The question echoes across millennia (maybe eons, if we had the sense, or the collective humanity, to detect the reverberation across so vast a plane of memory): What is poetry?

From brutes and bards and Beatniks have come many answers, some with rhyme and reason, and others in a waterfall of square definitions for round terms the neat categories that Rationalism and logic demand.

But typically, definitions of what poetry is – whether written or read aloud or sounded in the symphonic silence of the mind – have shared common descriptive elements. Poetry is an oddly fleeting but stable and durable cloud, a flower, and an assertion and affirmation of beauty. Poetry is admission, passion, outrage, revelation, declaration, exhortation, rejoicing, mourning, desire, triumph, and surrender. It is love. Poetry is life, scrawled and spoken.

Poetry is the discernible – the perceptible, the felt – connection of the human mind and heart and soul to the range of human emotion that can be expressed in words. Poetry is power – absolute, unbridled, and unashamed, but controllable and, often, healing. It is naked emotion; it is the whopping yet strangely subtle Moksha from the mundane for people attuned to feel it. Poetry is emotions painted in words that score soul song meant to cause motion in the body, the mind and the heart – to release and to liberate and to comfort us. Poetry is transformative.

Many of us who gladly struggle to define poetry – when we care to – also call it a never-ceasing search for truth.

These elements jump up and soar in the work of Christine O'Leary-Rockey. She is a poet of passion and panache, a keen observer of the human condition who has the wordsmithing prowess to describe that condition in revealing, startling, and unforgettable imagery, and in turns of phrase that demand to be considered.

O'Leary-Rockey's poetry is infused with blood, sweat, tears, vigor, joy, and happiness, and with reverence and irreverence. Her poetry is alive with the power and the weakness and the salvation and the slavery of religion; with a wonder of living and loving; with a sense of the self-killing onus of servitude to many masters, and with the ecstasy of emancipation from one or all; with defiance and acceptance; with sarcasm and succor and tenderness; and with anointing images from a wide and tender heart reacting to existence in rat-a-tat-tat and coolly quiet lines that will touch you in more ways than a ring-breeze will ever touch you.

So ask no more what poetry is. Come into the pages of Christine O'Leary-Rockey's The 3 Faces of Brahman and see – *feel* – what poetry is.

Bon voyage.

## *Michael Lear-Olimpi*

Michael Lear-Olimpi

*Poet and journalist*
*Adjunct Lecturer in Humanities, Elizabethtown College*
*Adjunct Lecturer in Humanities, Pennsylvania State University*
*Harrisburg, Pennsylvania, April 2010*

The 3 Faces of Brahman

## Contents

| | |
|---|---:|
| *Job Festered ...* | 1 |
| *The Wisdom of Delilah* | 11 |
| *Meditations on the Middle Class* | 12 |
| *Lacan's Dilemma* | 14 |
| *The Prostitute's Song* | 16 |
| *Irish Lace* | 17 |
| *Sarah's Burden* | 18 |
| *Stoning the Magdalene* | 19 |
| *Midwivery* | 22 |
| *Somnambulance* | 23 |
| *A Love Song in Gray Mourning* | 26 |
| *clouds for breakfast* | 27 |
| *There must be an inherent distrust of logjams* | 28 |
| *Concentric (or) Allah in Circles* | 29 |
| *Resurrection* | 31 |
| *Convoluted* | 32 |
| *Red Stockings* | 33 |
| *A Lullaby ...* | 35 |
| *Canary* | 36 |
| *St. Julian* | 37 |
| *Agave all in Red* | 39 |
| *Theos Ex Nihlim* | 40 |
| *Sonata 85* | 41 |
| *The 3 Faces of Brahman* | 43 |
| *Lolita in a Small Town* | 45 |
| *Journey to Siam* | 47 |
| *Local Gods* | 49 |
| *Pueblo* | 51 |
| *Electra: From the Closet* | 52 |
| *Lacan Pt. II. The Vacancy* | 54 |
| *Would it be disappointing...* | 55 |

THE 3 FACES OF BRAHMAN

## *The Wisdom of Delilah*

Pillows breed strange revelations, ones
I would not be caught
undressed in.  One never enters a bed
unarmed.

Truth cannot be your blanket: It is sheer and
heavy, weighs down the body.  It lets in the cold
and rain and the eyes of predators — both simple
and complex.  To be garbed
with truth makes you foolish like royalty —
an Emperor
wearing his kingdom's fortune
with pride. Love plays
these games, they're called: find the innocent — then we All
  S c a T te r —       Marco
              Polo

                          Marco
Polo
    Catch
the
         tiger
by the
                      Polo!
Caught by the hair— dragged before jackals in iron mail:
Love's fool pride leading man before vanity's precipice.

I tell you:
Samson deserved to lose his eyes.

## *Meditations on the Middle Class*

I do not know where these images come from,
only where they go — into the hole
with the credit cards and light bills.
The little black box that sings Beethoven
has become an umbilical cord to you.
Its chirping sweetly reminiscent
of a repeating decimal
that will never quite equal one.

So I curse — and repeat the question:
How can one become wise from taking a life
when I have not grown wise by giving it?

A question that thrusts me into path of gravity,
up the wall to the window,
forcing me to grab onto the nearest solid object

which brings me back to you.

Behind this window, solipsism is the possible
as all things drift and move within. Rain, cars,
pavement spreading like a scab, the wound large
reaching for the comb of trees,
eating the dawn and shitting out
the thick, raw black.
All of this is but reflection, not of the out
but the in: There is another world
another and another — one with many children,
and a car that doesn't move.
A heroin habit, there is one filled with thick silence
and the sound of whiskey in the kitchen.
Ice
and bleached hands.

From this room, solipsism is a possible
rite of passage just when all things seem machine.
Footsteps passing like birds passing like cars passing
like clocks striking clocks striking birds striking cars the cars
they rock me
to dreaming ...

Our lack of contact with each other
allows us to become what we fear —
cold.
Relational with the mirror.
Seducing ourselves
with images
of a risen Christ.

## The 3 Faces of Brahman

### *Lacan's Dilemma*

We are in process. Yeah —
that's the ticket …
Lacan is bringing about a revolution — a transfiguration —
a recreation of a new social possibility and he's doing it all
without the help of the holy host. Ssssssh!
 Instead, he's using language. The application of the I.
The origin of mirror play and the cracks that exist
between the statement "I want a cookie"
and the desire to actually eat one …

mmmm. They're so yummy.
Cookie Monster is the beginning face of ideological hegemony
and the chosen social ill. Yeah, the big CM is a tool of
"The Man."
When we are young we learn what happens
when desire goes wild — those crumbs — they go flying.

The objectification of the subject
breeds schizophrenia — then hides the dance
beneath the allegory of Freudianism and a big skirt.
Tells us that to be woman is to have a predilection for food
and a constant lack. Of friends. Of choice. Of penis. Of self-esteem.
Only woman can pose and trump, only woman can gossip or
weep. To be woman is to be victim
and victim is that which is without the ever-potent stiffy…
Yeah …
That's language too.

Perhaps Derrida would have argued — the self
is only the posit. The first shock of awareness
over the face in the mirror
and the refusal to spend your life aware
of another repeating, mocking, mimicking everything you do.
You must incorporate your reflection
or face life against your own strange polarity.

It is harder to embrace that stranger
when she's telling lies.
When she's the one everyone likes/hates/fears/wants
objective/subjective self sitting home alone while the reflection
cavorts on butterfly-style.

Woman *is* dichotomy. Subjective/objective, to hear
expectations spoken and be told
they are your own. To be told what you think, what you
hear, how you move
and be corrected for thinking
that you somehow extend beyond your body
into the great Everything.
and that on Judgment Day
you will hand God back your skin and say,
Thanks, lord, I'm done with it now.
And still be you.

Vagina-less. Without the hips. Same eyes.

## The 3 Faces of Brahman

### *The Prostitute's Song*

If you knew the years I spent pulling you from my veins.
The blood lost — opening my arms and lying still
waiting for your vapor to seek the slits you loved
and escape into the air,
'cause I always pictured you, your presence, wrapped around me
woven through my nerves
burlap-style.

I could see you in the darkness,
your shadow across my floor.
It became the thing under my bed —
Hidden. Grotesque, far more frightening when I couldn't find it
than when I did.

I have grown used to paying for my life with my body.
I have grown tired
of paying for my life with my body.
It has always been my need
to pay.
Broken bottles bite upon this bitter need to break
to break
to bury itself shoulder deep
and declare the world a war.

I am the light, the truth and The Way.
I am the cripple born on this day.
I am the apple once fell from the tree.
I am the fallen, my Lord, Glory be....

## *Irish Lace*

Her bags sit packed, pastels
waiting as if she had rifled through them yesterday
and were but a movement away

waiting, on the brink of her room
where the dark is tense.
But the smell of her dying is the only ghost
and it is tangible. Not the friend I had
hoped for.

Now is why we created ghosts, to preserve our love.
Even if from a gray nether-world, we pretend
their eyes are upon us,
the imagination of ghostly unknowns
better than the certainty of gone.
Death leaves its reminders
anew, clothing in drawers,
a scent upon their clothes, defying
us to believe.

## THE 3 FACES OF BRAHMAN
### *Sarah's Burden*

Round and
firm
    protective as any mother,
I tenderly wait for this thing
to be.
To somehow unfold, to open itself
and cry.

I wonder
   if I will know it
   or love it.
I wonder
    on its face and eyes
and which body parts I will count ...

Already I know
    it will have my eyes
    and thin hands
that will look like mine as mine are
my mother's.
It will laugh at private things
   and have many appetites,
   many needs — this thing.
   Parasite or higher
it may transform me or leave
me dry.
Our children are meant to surpass,
to correct our twists and be strong
where we are weak...

.... Maybe a child
or a snake ....
Mother or host ...
but this I know:
Some things must chew
their way outside.

## *Stoning the Magdalene*

There is no honor in this/ Not in these bells
that sob with the voice of swallows.
Armed and naked I rise,
mouthing mantric circles to creatures of air
and blood. The world was set to spin
just so.

Not like us. These denizens of the small places
hold their own — there is much earth provided,
but with such clear waters who needs
the sun- its viscous alacrity shining
when the moon dips, giving its penny blonde face
mountains of its own.
Not like mine, poor bartered soil.

All of this, and Cassiopeia too —
hardly scared now. The dragon never made it.
Even her father drifts in his chair.
Only the wife remains. Frightened and stiff, looking
at fleeing before the next comet may (not) arrive
but only pass — taking her hope, her freedom, her
need for dragons
and daughters
away.

II.

The stars remain
unnatural altars, ever twisting like wraiths
and doves — those little songs of mourning w/no real meat...
But us — we eat them anyway. It is what we
do, we pick their bones as our lives,
not for ourselves but others, especially when they intrude
and die for us.
What is one cross vs. another but blame
laid decisively low and lacking direction?
This is the pattern we see
when we cast our stones at each other.
Not shadows, ellipses or
sly creatures — simply a truth
that cannot be riddled away.

## The 3 Faces of Brahman

Not while spinning poetic silhouettes
that insist they will exceed us.  Do they
not? They exceed us
like the ocean's wide brim
that eats sailors.  And ships.  Even the sky
I'm told sometimes folds itself like a fan
into gently flooded hills
where the dolphins  (yes, the dolphins …
It would have to be the dolphins
since the merfolk are all gone now,
leaving just you
and me
because the merfolk are all gone now —
It's just you and me
'cause the merfolk are nothing
if not dead.)

Which is okay, you know.
There is no better place than one that cradles you
fondly to and fro, so you know
they're being loved so soundly
that the gulls must SHOUT them
awake.  The sea eats its folk- the
fish are like candy, caramel goblins and
eels breed in places we've only spoken of.
The ocean holds them in its mouth
like brown sugar and marbles — Oh, do be careful
you don't choke on my goblins or other silica gods

or angels, swimming in the water
and rooting in deep caverns.  We are to
pull ourselves, we are to pull ourselves — we are
too tired to pull ourselves
from the water to air.  Feet make poor fingers.
We need them to run and
to swim.  We run.  From ourselves, we run.
It is only at a distance I see you, bluely
and unpresent.
It must be you
because only one reflection sings that way

and it is not yours.  Or anyone's
for that matter.  And it
does matter, does it not?

Lying about in the great absurdity of it all?
I've never believed in angels. Or corals, for that.
They are too frail, wound in threads
nothing I know of spins. Spinning is an art.
Ask any Scorpion and we'll deny our tapestries
to the uninitiated, the uninvited. Yet, even as we are weavers
sometimes we are caught
and that is where I am. Not.
But on your shore

straining to feel Calypso's pure note
as she pours it through the wind
and water, into the bones
of the sea.

## The 3 Faces of Brahman

### *Midwivery*

It was always the stone between us — red
speaking, white speaking
things in shells and half-baked pies.
There were ants in those cupboards
and witches nearby.

We needed a bed — one for the water
to wear away, for the creatures
to hunt by.
But we begged instead for language.
As if words were crow bait — as if
shaping vowels
or the act of passing on the act
of passing on were anything
but the act
of passing on.
What did the wild nature bring us
in its hounds and bansidhe hair
but summer things — cherry stones
blood columbine,
birthing and reaffirming death
in its wonderful fruition.

## *Somnambulance*

It can be said that she
Mother of Other Worlds
wept
at the face of that omen.
Buried her face in the sheets
that blinded the world
held her whimpers
and her climax.
It all came to her in a moment
that it was
too far.
There was too much
between the melody and the words.
All are smooth ravings, all are
the songs of the unexpected
dead.

(Where do we bury them?
The moaners, the talkers —
the ones who rattle dry arms
plumbing the darkness/For sound.)
They whisper secrets into the ear
of prowling night
while we roll in fits and
starts
Dreaming their round voices
and hearing the face
of the shouting dead.

      II.

Spuriously
    this protean
        sleeps
      in a
    small
   blue ball
by my window.

Shape shifter —
Woman with a hundred faces —
none of you is real.

## The 3 Faces of Brahman

You know this
as you plunge your hands
into the soft gray nape of the sky.

You breed poppies
as pets, unfolding their white palms
as they cock their heads at the sun.
Arrogant.
The way Ladies
and stewards
are.

The pearls at your throat are soft.
They speak silver
to the shadows.
To the darkness …
In the darkness …
For the darkness
all circles believe themselves
to be moons …

She tells me —
I can weep you a keeper
or sew you a man
while her hands flutter on — weaving thistles from ash.
Even pearls are but gray stones
      when the moon is nestled
         deep in the spine of the sky
    that mirrors as mercury
and moves like old blood.

    III.

The air is cold.
It populates your eyes with the breathing
of mountains and snow.
Whispers gather in the eddies between trees
clattering like geese — murmuring on about battles
and lost brides.

Where is the division btw' the hero
and his fall?
What line does one cross when seeking
the revulsion

the revolution
which will win back the steed, re-forge the weapon
and fodder the aching hillside?
They gather, these ghosts
and parlay their loves and their horses.
They throw stones and roll bones
drinking blood from the pheasants
that hide
in the rushes.
Each one saying:
"My bride was the loveliest of them all ..."

The truth is this:
All men dream themselves heroes when they molder —
but for most, courage is first born
when their dust mingles with the quartz
and dead leaves.

Yes. Here all souls can be brave —
They shake *their* hair
to send foxes running.
Rolling their bones, wagering a traveler's spoils,
they are lifting our tresses toward the dark line of trees
tugging our locks.
One more roll, my lad,
before we push you back out into the black
where the wolves become mendicants
and thieves.

## The 3 Faces of Brahman

### *A Love Song in Gray Mourning*

Blue is for your eyeballs. They are gray
and frequently foggy.
I have not seen you in a fortnight
and drink to you often. That is how we see best.
I wore the scarf at my neck to remind me
of how you untied it. I didn't wind it
very hard.

Blue is for your weathervane, the thumbnail
that wouldn't break,
and other cosmetic impossibilities.
The wind blew again last night
and for the first time
I wasn't afraid.
She has stolen you already …
why fear anything moving away?

Blue is the open hand, the way
your eyes curve and do not land. It's the
feet that stumble and the steps
that always fall. Blue is a mantle
and your mantra. It's for the smoky air
and the sickly-sweet odor of every deer I've seen
lying bloated on the highway.
For baby's breath,
and the ones who never come.
For stillness
and that place we are
between breathing.

I could still my heart once — pause it
till my head rang.
I do that now
and pretend it is the sound
of you shouting.

### *Clouds for Breakfast*

The roses slid their fingers through air. Change
the only mathematical constant/like
sea serpents and lost boys

We use flowers to describe absence
affronted by negative space/emptiness
is a breath — let go/nature abhors a vacuum
and we create them

I am brittle on the edges, broken at the core
but as buttress against order — there I am brick
my skeleton is stronger than I am/the rest of me
is cloud

# The 3 Faces of Brahman

## *There must be an inherent distrust of logjams*

Trying to explain the refractory nature of light
and its electromagnetic passions
to the cynical, unsmiling eyes of a boy who is not yet 13
is fundamentally flawed.

All things will unveil themselves in time.
It is the nature of things to unmask the phenomenon
of all faces given place given unbroken unsmiling
movementnotmovement or the thrust within the shadow.
All things speak your face. If not yours
then the face you might have been.
It is not too late to show your heel
as a willing participant in The Way.

It says Solomon dressed in lilies: We know that is false.
He wore silk and his queens
very little
but he supped for the Lord
and blessed Him just the same.

Of course you bleed — it is the way of things.
Like mountains that bite
and rocks that fumble their way through the sky.

Freedom weighs only on the animals that know.
That would be us.
And God has not died for white heron,
or haven't you read that yet?

I have. Mix it with white gold
and the movement of Nietzsche's watch.
You'll find all things come unglued
if watched longly.
Just wait, I tell you:
Being will unveil its face like a bride.

# Concentric
## (or)
# Allah in Circles

If God is an algorithm
        as you swore one night between us
then heaven must surely exist two steps from
  H E R E
Beginning broken and chaotic
its equations curling as snowflakes and stairwells do.
    And I wonder if all algorithms are truly coloric
— Color being purely a myopic thing — unspokenly linked
to those places
in the black of your eyes.

Perceptually in transit we are not
capable of true motion. Heraclitus said
the river always changes
so we sat beside it and watched
'til no serpent's back broke the stillness of its flow
to challenge this change, forcing sameness by presence
that knows
no static bounds.

If Heraclitus was indeed on target —
that all motion is true motion and there is only motion —
then that would explain God's inconsistency
and his damned fickle behavior.
We *can* go on.
But if we don't we are bound by this puzzle
and its superstitious need
to get beyond space and into the realm of sound.  And color.

To end this mystery here:
There is no more — color.
It is no more real than sound or love or metaphysics.
And if a tree fell in the forest
nobody would give a damn.

Not if they knew.  Know they now?  Thyself
to whit — there are no revelations. Not in sound or color.
No, if He speaks, he speaks in numbers.
In negatives and symbolic logic. Logarithms that go squawk
in the night.

# The 3 Faces of Brahman

His movement — at one hundred gyrations per second —
lulls our perfect senses
into a sense of time/no time/timelessness ...
We mistake this movement for song.

We perceive radiation only. Its bright millobars blind us
as passionate reflection;
so do we tout the brocaded sky, serendipitously black and shredded
each embedded icicle in perfect relation
               to the one behind it, around it — the cool red
            the white hot
     the perfect seeds far off and away
are dull repeated patterns that fit just so
into our little keyholes — though these tones exist only as
electromagnetic gray.

Sound and color.  God help us, sound and color.
To sense is to translate, each tap a nudge to real numbers.
Vastly we calculate, we react and transcribe.
God may be lost there, hiding w/in the physicist's dark matter,
but truly He left us pieces of his tools.

We are linked
body to mind.
We are one soul — we chemical dreamers —
charming the snake of physicality.

## *Resurrection*

He cracked my head — that's when it all
spilled out — the wresting, the waiting
and weight of wasted time.

These days
I measure the Holy
by the length of its shade.
I never did see the difference
between an empty space
and a shrine.

> *Come — sit with me amidst the blood and shadows*
> *and tell my why you hurt so.*
> *I've played this fiddle before*
> *but now I can handle the bow.*

By God, but it draws me forward —
beyond this frozen plain —
head down — lips parted and dry.

The day belongs to he who spins it
spade in hand, brown skin
patient in bronze — all things eventually go
underground.
Even me, he says.
He calls it
Easter.

I ask you again:
How much does your redemption weigh?

> *So come — lie with me in the shadows*
> *and teach me how to go.*
> *I have played this fiddle before*
> *but now —*
> *now I can handle the bow.*

## The 3 Faces of Brahman

```
        D   C
      E       O
    T           N
      E       V
        T   O
        U   L
```

The way it all c o m e s
rushing back

Everything is purged: Ares has swept through
and you are the new god, the alpha and
the old.

You are the maven, I
the whore.
The setting — Rome,
and we stand across the sand.

All things in circles —
Mantras, pollen, ammonites.
Semiotics speaks of the arcs of language
and gender
weaving like trout,
each meaning hatching from its airborne seed
Worlds are born from just one misplaced
sound — night/day/night/day/night
and day again.

## *Red Stockings*

Upon meeting her
one gets the feeling that she is in constant dialogue.
With you — you expect — until you realize
she's not there.
As if the words she says to you are distractions
from the ongoing conversation she's holding with herself
and whatever world
she's in.

It's not just the words — watch
and you'll see her lips moving while in the shopping aisle
behind the car, in her rear view mirror. As if
those unfocused looks are somehow the whole of it
and you're only there occasionally —
a ripple in the fabric of her dream.

There are many like that. For these
the silent tipping of the second hand is fluid
and carries the pattern of a dance. Its dizzy path dips and claws,
stretching like a marshmallow when time is soft
and the world around is crunchy with detail.
Those times.

Others too.
The clock shows itself the animal it is
by laying temperamentally in the archway.
Then the wind casts lots into the picture — her arms
suddenly reach — Christ-like — to fly. One day.
It will be thrilling.
As every dream was before she stopped dreaming. Or flying.
Or whatever it was that left her clinging
to the ground so tightly.

But we all start small.
Ashes-to-ashes, we all fall prey
to predatory logic;
raging at hands that never hold still.
The tragedies are:
love,
suicide
and the rituals of time.

## The 3 Faces of Brahman

Truth is something to be gotten over.
You can't *live* by her.

But she IS there. Hanging alongside doorjambs and old signs.
She is often shabby and dressed like a whore.
Only when you buy her wares do you open her up
seeing her from the inside.

Hence the conversation: a courtship ritual.
Like any lady, one must court her often
not leave her unattended too long.

But what do you do when she wakes you
in the middle of the night when nobody stirs?
What will you do?

You don't.
You light a candle
watch its shadows on the wall.

You don't.
You light a candle
and watch it burn.

## *A Lullaby ...*

Sleep now, my ponies, my babies, my lives
Mamma's little baby gonna lay down and die
Just for the morrow, just for the nigh'
Mamma's so tired she just gotta fly ...

Hush now, my babies, my ponies, my loves
The evening's a sinister whisper of wings
Ssssh, now, my lovers, my babies, my doves
Night times a'calling in the voices of things
long time not spoken, long how not heard
Evening is dressed in the throat of a bird
hidden in leeway, tumbled in stone
Evening's the lover that went on alone
waltzing in tune under bent sky
Velvet blue sheath, she danced on a sign
of horizon that spread 'pon the earth like a song ...

Evening lasted that night very long ...

Her flowers were music, her perfume
a glove, the nectar of night was the fruit
of her love.  Moving around a fixed ancient stone
rocking her hips, her breast all along
to measure the carving, mouthing rune song
in love with the night sky nine hundred mile long ...
See bats in attendance, king moon — it is grand
A court of the hilltops that could weep on command
Weaving and praising, she prayed on the hill
The velveteen woman, she's praying there still
For the stars to be ice, for the mountains to glisten
For the caribou child, the wolves' lullaby
— listen —
Rolling off of the rock shires, the tops of the mounts
Ringing 'cross treetops and shaking the fonts
at the root of the mountains, the skirts of the shore
Our ritual mistress,
the Mother of More ...

## *Canary*

Today is the day to write you a letter
if only to begin again.
Thick as blood. I saw you when you were dreaming —
and nodded as if to say: This way.
I have created you This Way — against both of our will.
I, mine, yours, ours, we lie beautifully
and play Prophet in each act of rising ...
then fall ...

I sat and wrote you a letter today
but penned no words. Not this time.
There were too many places for the words to run —
mirrors with sharp edges and
dirty fingers. Their shy ghosts nudging
me for a penny. Instead I am purging — purging
your figure, purging your face — purging the futures you
placed in the air. Oh, my Gemini, I'm so glad you've awakened.
I just wasn't ready for the cold.

I called to you today, but made no
sound — it would have disturbed the water,
the fabric of the trees. Still, the birds exploded
as if lighter than before.
But I kept one
and have given her your name ...

And now I'm burning your letters — burning your pen,
each page becoming in heat and color
what it never was
in hand.

> "The Trinite is our maker and keeper, the Trinite is our everlasting lover, everlasting joy and blisse, be our Lord Jesus Christ; and this was shewed in the first... And I said, 'Benedicite, Domine.'"
>
> ### *St. Julian of Norwich*

If only Julian could dream, and in that dream
she wept roses
rising from snow the way stalkers
and lovers do.
She would flee their fair lips, round and
engorged. Supple with sex that succumbs
to the bleeding of bedrolls, and biscuits —
the hard round body of Christ
administered by pimps
and misfits.

If only Julian could weep, and in her weeping ran wild
racing the gauntlets of flesh, the heat of
the day, her tears not pearls, as the Lord promised,
but stones
killing The Magdalene.
Smashing her skull, the beautiful
lips that spoke woman
on the Sabbath.
The righteous are free
to kill.
Julian knows this
because she runs from them

in her dreams where they hunt her
pack-like, driving from field to stone,
voices baying through mansions and valleys

where she wakes within holy walls.
Here, the cattle dogs let her be, the
hunters, the wolves
in priests' clothing.
She utters her communion, white shift heavy
upon her body
burning for the Christ
as promised.
She would have Him.

## The 3 Faces of Brahman

And in her visions, He comes

wooing her with gifts of fever
and thorn.
In the dark of the day,
always in stone,
He comes.

Triune and alive.

## *Agave all in Red*

Pyrotechnically borne to be the mouthpiece of Allah.
He is God, the old God, Ares of the field
and sheets.
Scented and grim,
with all of the beauty a dark djinn brings ...

Wine — I offer you wine, Lord. Pungent and
old, in casks of blood and flour.
Your birds are split, the hour is cold
and we have grown old, my lord.
oh, how we have grown old ...

The world is young, yet
never so. In it, we are young, yet
never so. In love with birds and
bodies spread like manure to water the fields.
Destruction takes the face of a boy.
Creation another.
Soon they wander, their
footsteps leaving pools
where the river gods dwell.

Your altar is here
waiting.
Sacrifices are started:
The blood is still warm.
Revelry has come. It is Spring
and it is time to ride the bull to the mountain.

I will ride you and your many hands, your
eyeless revelry.
Your maids will know me,
and we will ride this bull to the mountain.

The wheel must turn.
It comes on the shoulders of the massive
and the male,
where the wine is the year, the new wine.
The pantheon will follow.
And we will ride this bull to the mountain, my Lord.
We will ride this bull to the mountain ...

## The 3 Faces of Brahman

### *Theos Ex Nihlim*

As a writer who has never lived in Europe
I must write about America — as if it's possible
to be an exile in a land of waylaid travelers.
Solidity is the first thing to go
if you are to swing about
in the great exhale of sky.
There is one breath.
It roars continuously, causing the trees to shake.

That must be where you've gone —
under the leaves with the lions.

To see you would be to change my
perspective, give you a place in my dreams.
Quick as a whip
your words are forgotten, your tongue
now a whirlwind
into the earth-baked ground.

If I wrote to you, it could change my perspective,
place you into my dreams — a place
I could reach, a skin I could make real. But
you are not reachable. Nor real.

These are the secrets between us — slight obstacles
and electric. Simmering between
as aroma.  We have promised not to mention
anythingnothingeverything
and there is nothing as long as we pretend

well. That I am not missing a face I once wrote,
pretend I'm not aching a need to speak.
Missing a voiceless face and repeating a name
with no connection. Love
without passion. A face without mystery.
Haunted by casualness, so reluctant to
move my pen.

There is a window within which
all colors can be seen.
This poem is about nothing
if not forgiveness.

## Sonata 85

For this grand song, time paces itself
brusk like a wooden runner
it marches on — common nods proclaim
drum beat drum beat drum beat on
each hard/footstomp/razorthickblackboot
stomp/ss/bastard/forward

But for this my gentle one, bringing kindness to my own
eyes — they crinkle upon you — knowing your sound and
the rich fine timbre of your sweetness.
Green I say to you — blue you answer — both we know
these colors spend royal like lovers on horses
silver in wind — a song before summer
sand before rain, bells upon a holy Easter morn ...

Yeah. I would pray with you. 'Tis time we reconstitute God.
To let him out of his dark prison — ask Him if He's ready
to love us yet.
He will laugh with us, with His white teeth flashing/ Such
a fine God He is, dressed in His best hat and fiddle.
My grandfather wore a hat like that before he died — he too
was class and I think that now He
dresses God just for me
so we will know each other.
Meet like strangers, part like lovers,
our ways foreign to a mortal
child — but lovers aren't mere children they are past

that. They have gone beyond and have become shy.
For this we pity/love them, we envy/hate them, we
all wish we could be them
only sometimes.

We are better than lovers, better than hazelnuts
yeah — branches over
the widest of places and
our roots entwine.
Even the frozen stream may pale — we are stronger.
We are November dwelling in soil and dead cicadas.

## The 3 Faces of Brahman

Sleep, slight green thing, willow on the eastern shore.
When you wake it will be to spring — fair lady.
Autumn sweeps sudden past — heavy orange and red.
She is proud and hard to reach. She is
haughty, she is
so fond
of green apples.

## *The Three Faces of Brahman*

Her blue eyes jut forward now —
fishlike — liquid bubbles each cell
rod cones capillaries backwards- bowing inward to the very core
while tied to the hub — an almighty ball that copulates with itself
within.

But it is my movement that is artificial, as are
all of my motions: Walking, speaking, the way I hold
my pen.
These things have become grounded,
not as earth —
but in the way planes fall out of the sky.

Watching is not so much pain as process.
Like writing this poem — only half my attention is here ...
My own needs continue to tap their foot — successfully
sometimes.

So I'm braking for ice cream, my hands are too tight
to write much less hang onto this wheel.
My words are tight/my stomach/my breathing is tight
as if wracking my chest with dry heaves ...

Maybe someday this will be a poem ...

God help us both when she's awake,
watching my every move — her watery eyes
gone stiff — cellophane on the white linen of her face.
Her fingers are a girl's, rattling the rail, chanting
help me help me help me
I ask how.
Sometimes
she'll meet me in the eye.
Says, I don't know.
Please, she says,
help me.

# The 3 Faces of Brahman

She'll say, I'm so happy to see you.
Please, I'm so happy to help you.
Please I'm happy, I'm so help me, I'm so help me please …
Help me, help me help me …

The odor creeps down the corridor on feet she'll never use,
the pungent dance of shit and ammonia. Of plastic wrappers
and terrified young nurses.
She squeezes my hand
and holds it 'till my side aches.
But I — I want to sit. I am horrified at how I want to sit
but I so need to sit
while some blind parasite
quietly consumes her brain.

When this is done she will be just bone
and saliva.


I tell my Lord that he is a bastard
and a thief
before he catches me,
saying

he must coax the flesh to let go.

Nine months in the shaping.
A small eternity in the brine where we move
from fish to frog to anonymous creation —
then eighty years of holding our breath
and refusing
to let it go.

It's no wonder she lies now
shaking the walls.

## *Lolita in a Small Town*

Occidental/oriental —
Symbolism is knowledge transcending experience
metaphors are truths
gone underground ...

This one whispered: Anything in a man's world
then it closed
the door.

Witch hazel in a jar. A withered mandrake
the yellow — black pique of your eyes.
Fluttering curtains and a passionate breeze
cannot disguise a gradual suicide ...

Let me tell you a secret:
I am only brave until the body
goes
down.

No, I am the woman
who throws herself onto the coffin.

Who has followed the moment into nothingness
and lies awake, dry-eyed and sedated.
The one who refuses to live.

Only the faces change.
Some more interesting, more assuming,
some more clandestine than
others.

I'd step out of my skin
if I could,
drape it across the chair.
Let you wrangle to your
hearts'
content.

While I'm elsewhere
swimming in an oasis
where the water doesn't run for you.

## The 3 Faces of Brahman

You are the same — you are
no different
than the first man who spread my legs
or the last.

## *Journey to Siam*

Yes, your Gemini occupies my daily
thought, the empty chair. Even
an occasional dream.
This would please you I know
but it cannot please you too much.
Haunting is your word, but it implies
frequency, and your erraticism is disorienting.
It creates its own direction
and I am drawn to your shores
by way of the river. You would be pleased

and few things please you. Perhaps

this is good, this hide and seek — too many
make themselves obvious — a cardinal sin:
The fat man with the belly shirt — the
need to see when you would rather not
believe. You're subtlety is intriguing,
but I have broken masks before.
And I am more interested in the composition of your bricks
than in the rooms of your house, more
curious of your strengths than your sin,
and enough of a sinner
that I am not afraid.

Didn't I know you
somewhere that isn't here
and isn't that why I feel your eyes upon me,
decipher your symbols so well?
Brotherloverhusbandpriest you/we are all both/neither.
We are Gemini entwined
and once upon a time
I loved you.
This I know.
That is why your siren

calls. I shut my ears but
stay bound.
You are too deep, my one.
And I know if I step into the sea
you will leave me there
to drown.

 THE 3 FACES OF BRAHMAN

How sad it would be to destroy your shadow.
To fracture your whole; to lose yourself
anew.
I am pearl, you wood — together
we are complete,
the circle our God started
before we were
born.

## *Local Gods*

They are the creations of a thousand nights' passion —
oft' regretted, sometimes restored.
Each cherub stone, figurine
receives our light and darkness, imagined fealty
and the loyalty we reserve for ourselves.
So let us lay them in webs
and meshings.
Let us layer them under a thousand excuses
and light a candle
to pray they spare us
the pain
of the harvest moon.

They need a new name —
One whispered into cats' ears, to virgins in red silks
their lovers gone, spindled legs
totter as young spiders in the dark ... stumbling
toward the old Gods.

But sex is the alter of the Scorpion
and Power be our God.
Equality for Libra
but mortal be our sod.

Only here can I offer comfort
and the knowledge that you seek.
I offer you my stories
and the wisdom of the weak.
I offer you the mendicant
and the hanged man.
I offer you totality
that only other can.

Here I am a demon ship
upon a mighty sea —
and carry naught but souls
around, around- around around
the nautical IS she goes
as child's toy or winding brace
which tore the trees in whole —
I have your soul upon my face

**The 3 Faces of Brahman**

and return it to you seven-fold.
But you cling the boards a drowning man
with more fear of the sea
than me.

Swim, dammit!
You can.

## *Pueblo*

This movement is
coming.
This motion is
flowing, the delta is
too close.
I think it's time to run again.

Haven't done it, now it's time
to hide, away from all the words
I've used. To get under
the bed, go into the closet.
She never found me in the closet.
I have always felt safe
in small places.
This think is big — it is bigger than
me, I think. This ledge is looming
larger than buffalo. This is where
they rush them off the cliff,
this is where they slashed their palms.
This is where the prints
stand
still.

I am not bigger. I am not braver.
I am not anything
other than the little thing he calls me,
and I don't know
if I can continue to think this way.
'Cause his antennae are in my head:
Loosespeak, the words with many
meanings — as opposed to Tightspeak,
the place with only one.
Yours is scalpel done.
This time, I want to see it
with the ashes rubbed
inside.

## The 3 Faces of Brahman

### *Electra: From the Closet*

My father is leaving the green land,
leaving his ruined castles, traveling on
to where he and my mother can't live together
anymore.
I tell her that there are only ten stories
and they do not change much.
She tells me I am a cynic and moves on.

The diabetes makes him stumble. That and the vodka.
They were both there when he fell through the table
feeding the scarabs that scramble his veins like red spiders.
As a child he told me scarabs were sacred.
That must be why he fights so hard to keep them.

We both fear madness.
The kind that drove his father mountains away
looking for — nothing. But he *was* looking for something.
So the old stumble from the crowd to seek their memories,
their visions cut them from the herd like wolves.
The Inuits let themselves freeze. It is kinder
than the way we rot from the toes or lungs out.
Each culture has its stories. I have mine. Some are about drinking,
others suicide, but really they are the same story.

The same woman is born again and again and again ...
She comes from the water, but not all of us can swim.
Some are too heavy, others cold.
We move lemming-like across the cliff,
geology becoming important
only on the way down.
It's what we forget until we too fall off the stone face
and into the story of what was.
Our fathers birth us a second time, often by sword.
Ipheginia. Red Ridinghood. Both were set free.
See?
This is the same story, the same woman.
The endings never change.

We only pretend to live together. Proximity is everything.
We fill in the cracks with chatter.

Whiskey is best for burying people,
beer for telling tales.
My father is Irish, so he does both.
It started when he cut his brother from the ceiling.
That's when the stories began to spill. They flowed
long after he buried him ... they flowed ...
Even now, they run
on vodka and water,
they run.

Perhaps there is no end. Perhaps
you have to finish the tale
or let go of the man
before you can put the glass
down.

## *Lacan Pt. II.*
## *The Vacancy*

To posit, oh posit oneself before language,
stripping oneself clean of all society
and murmur as a bird —
A hop and a peck, a signifier and
the worm. To be a bird
is to have been caught in the act
of signifying a song
in the imagination of a man.

A struggle with the phallus — every child's destiny,
to function as lack or as the answer to a need.
Suicide becoming just another possibility
a gray landscape of undifferentiated moon
in which we stumble.

If I greet your lack with bounty
does your opposing self slip into undeniable *ovtoð*?
Or create some new crack to redefine it in its loss?
We fade into new animals, some not yet born, by the advent of desire
and the fulfillment of its seventh task-
the ameleorization of the self
and all its blankets …

Subject/object subject/object.subject/object
I am between subject/object.
I am cold and because I know I am cold I am objectifying my subject,
but the sensual registration of cold may resolve itself
as desire, once again creating a subject.
I am individual only in my need.

So what is it to be filled?
If fulfillment is found in your arms
am I then creating myself and my lack
through your other?

Maya brought rain, Shiva the sound.
Buddha reads of the negation of the self
and is therefore undefined, undesired, unneeded,
while Jesus stamped the coin of the Western self,
spawning an unending psychic need to flagellate
and forgive.

***Would it be disappointing to watch the rain on a deserted corner in a former eastern block country if the coffee in your hand was too cool to warm your palms? It's been said that Marxism/Leninism/Communism stopped working when the hot plates produced only lukewarm coffee and the gulags were full ... Subsisting on only the bitter leaves of cabbages moves from sustenance to insult when man is deprived of heat — even in the most basic of ways. Prometheus was a hero only in that he was looking for a warm place to spend the night.***

Language is habit.
We know physicists use the notes of a color scale
to read the statement of a star.
Chemists burn metal.
All language. No language. Misleading, isn't it?
I'm using language to mislead even now
by pretending that I am doing something but pushing buttons.
I'm fortunate that you may recognize the patterns.
What is fascinating is that one dream
may be draped over so many souls.

Translation is where it all happens.
A slippery mess of wants, of insistences of one's own psyche
going forward like the hounds of war.
These canines, unleashed,
spread an array of linguistic violence
including the obliteration of nuance, conversion of multiplexity
and the funeral of the unconscious
by proclaiming the dirge of intentionality
while nipping at the heels of the lexicon —
(located right above the left ear.)
In it, Clydesdales tread solid over meaning, desire
and any implicit wish to welcome another's thoughts
into your own.

Instead, you release your own hounds
to clash in a bloody battle for truth
when in fact, she is hiding beneath the stair.

# The 3 Faces of Brahman

Your thoughts can no more mirror mine
than can the line of a ship mirror the surges of water.
It cuts through. It is utility only.
That and a futile need to dominate
the landscape.
We are better than nature — worse
than nature — our need for equilibrium is deep.
We are nothing without Harmony, even if it is found
in the banal

But the clock mutters red under it all
telling the world — I am all the time that matters.
Till once gone, babies get younger
trees block out fireworks once seen
in the park. Youth deceives us into making children
by giving us bodies that shine.
What were we thinking? That moment, that line, what were we
hoping? What we wore, what we
said ... Her glasses an out-of-date reminder
of the high school yearbook. Her three children
of the night she died.

We are midway through the time line
and declining.
Watching wild and beautiful
move into weight, alcoholism and Viagra.

What would you say
 if I told you that time was your friend?
That she moves about your bedroom
wearing your clothing when you shower?
What would you say if I told you
you should thank her
for carrying away the collagen
that supports your young skin and bad ideas ...
Or if I told you that we are pupae and
our lives never really begin
until we enter the web of middle age ...

Authenticity is artificial
unless you're willing to apply the knife
to the places that horrify you
the most.

I want colors
but cannot hold a tune long enough to learn the notes.
That would take time and I will not give it.
In case I fail.
In case I spend too long upon a problem
and find it looks like me.
In case I lack the colors, the casual sound,
the aptitude to set myself toward any real distinction.

I do
not
always matter to me,
only the refractions of my light —
chasing it as do ships a lighthouse —
not as warning
but instead
the signification
of stone.

## *About the Author*

Christine O'Leary-Rockey is a poet, writer and professor from Central Pennsylvania and is the author of one previous collection of poetry: <u>A Human Auction.</u> Her poetry and nonfiction has been published in a variety of regional and national publications, including <u>The Fledgling Rag</u>, <u>The Experimental Forest</u>, *Harrisburg Magazine, Central PA Magazine, Shirazad, Megaera, Haggard and Halloo* and others.

Christine holds a BS in Philosophy, and advanced degrees in Religion and Humanities, and currently teaches Humanities at Central Pennsylvania College in Summerdale, PA. In addition to performance, she has taught writing and performance workshops at St. Joseph's University, Philadelphia and for the Pennsylvania Student Press Association, and was a part of 2004's urban poetry expose, Open Stage Harrisburg's Court Street Poetry Jam. A two-time Harrisburg slam winner, Christine is a charter member of Harrisburg's infamous (almost) Uptown Poetry Cartel and was nominated for a Pushcart Prize in 2007.

www.ingramcontent.com/pod-product-compliance
Lightning Source LLC
LaVergne TN
LVHW051711080426
835511LV00017B/2856